MARC BROWN

ARTHUR'S FIRE DRILL

Random House 🏠 New York

Copyright © 2000 by Marc Brown. All rights reserved. Published in the United States by Random House Children's Books, a division of Penguin Random House LLC, New York. Step into Reading, Random House, and the Random House colophon are registered trademarks of Penguin Random House LLC. Arthur is a registered trademark of Marc Brown.

Visit us on the Web! StepIntoReading.com randomhousekids.com

Educators and librarians, for a variety of teaching tools, visit us at RHTeachersLibrarians.com

Library of Congress Cataloging-in-Publication Data
Brown, Marc Tolon.
Arthur's fire drill / by Marc Brown. p. cm. — (Step into reading. A step 3 sticker book)
Summary: Arthur helps ease D.W.'s fire fears by practicing fire drills at home.
ISBN 978-0-679-88476-7 (trade) — ISBN 978-0-679-98476-4 (lib. bdg.)
[1. Fire drills—Fiction. 2. Safety—Fiction. 3. Aardvark—Fiction.] I. Title.
II. Series: Step into reading sticker books. Step 3. PZ7.B81618 Apm 2003 [E]—dc21 2002013774

MANUFACTURED IN CHINA 20 19 18 17

When D.W. was a baby,
Arthur taught her
not to touch the hot stove.
"No!" he said. "Hot, hot!"

When D.W. was two years old,
Arthur taught her
about matches.
"No," he said.
"Never play with matches!"

Now D.W. is in nursery school.
Her teacher teaches her
all sorts of things…

how to tie her shoe,

how to print her name,

how to share.

One day the teacher said,
"Listen up, boys and girls.
Tomorrow we are going to have
a fire drill."

She told them what to do.
"When the fire bell rings,
stop what you are doing
and quickly line up at the door."

Then she took them outside.
"Now stop, drop, and roll
in the grass," she said.
They all stopped, dropped,
and rolled.

"This is fun!" said D.W.

"But what's it for?"

One of the Tibble twins said,

"It's if your clothes catch on fire."

"Oh!" said D.W. in a tiny voice.

That night D.W. whispered to Arthur,

"I'm not going to school tomorrow."

"Why not?" asked Arthur.

"There's going to be a fire," she said.

"You're making this up," said Arthur.

"Am NOT!" said D.W.

"Our teacher even

showed us what to do

when we catch fire tomorrow.

Stop! Drop! And roll!"

Arthur had to laugh.

"That's a fire DRILL,"

he said.

"It teaches you what to do
   if there ever is a real fire."
"I don't care what you say," said D.W.
"I'm not going to school tomorrow."

"I have an idea," said Arthur,
and he went into his closet.
When he came out, he gave D.W.
his play firefighter's hat
and a very loud whistle.

"We'll have a fire drill at home,"

said Arthur,

"and you can be in charge."

"Great!" said D.W.

"I get to be the fire boss."

"But first," said Arthur,

"you need to know the rules."

Arthur's Fire Safety Rules

☑ Don't hide. Get outside!

Never go back in.

☑ Stay low and go!

If you have to go through smoke,

put a wet towel on your head

and crawl out.

☑ Always use the stairs.

Never use the elevator.

☑ Be prepared!

Plan a way out now

with your family.

Always remember to first
get out of your house quickly.

Then go to a neighbor's house
to telephone the firehouse.

Just dial 911.

"Okay," said D.W. "I'm ready."

She ran down the stairs.

She blew her whistle. WHEEeee!

"Fire drill! Fire drill! Everyone out!

And don't forget Baby Kate,"

she shouted.

"WHAT!" said Dad.

"Just do what she says,"
said Arthur.

"She is the fire boss."

Pal ran out the door, and
the others quickly followed.
"What's all this about?"
asked Dad.
"It's D.W.'s homework,"
said Arthur.
"Tomorrow is her first fire drill."

D.W. had two more fire drills
that night.

"That's enough, D.W.," said Dad.

Then she made Arthur practice
how to get through fire or smoke.

"Hey! I'm all wet!"

shouted Arthur. "That's it!"

The next morning
D.W. was ready for school early.
But when she got there,
she saw a big red fire truck
out front.
"Oh, no!" she said.
"The school is on fire!
I need to get everyone out!"

Just then something strange
stepped out of the fire truck.
D.W. took one look at it
and screamed, "Help!
A monster!"

The strange thing said,

"Don't be afraid.

I'm not a monster.

I'm just a friendly firefighter."

And he took off his mask.

"See! This mask helps us

breathe in heavy smoke.

I'm here today to tell your class

how we fight fires.

Shall we go in?"

"I'll help, too,"

said D.W.

"I'm a fire boss."

After school,

Arthur asked D.W.,

"How was the fire drill?"

"No big deal,"

answered D.W.